big spring

big spring

elliot figman

four way books
new york city

Distributed by
University Press
of New England
Hanover and London

Editorial Office
Four Way Books
PO Box 535, Village Station
New York, NY 10014
www.fourwaybooks.com

Library of Congress
Catalog Card Number: 2002108345

ISBN: 1-884800-47-5

Book Design:
BRUNEL.

Cover Art:
PICABIA, Francis.
The Spring (La Source) (detail). (June-September) 1912.
Oil on canvas, 8' 2 1/4" x 8' 2 1/8" (249.6 x 249.3 cm).
The Museum of Modern Art, New York.
Eugene and Agnes E. Meyer Collection, given by their family.
Photograph ©2002 The Museum of Modern Art, New York.

This book is manufactured in the United States of America and printed on acid-free paper.

Four Way Books is a division of Friends of Writers, Inc., a Vermont-based not-for-profit organization. We are grateful for the assistance we receive from individual donors and private foundations.

Distributed by University Press of New England,
One Court Street, Lebanon, NH 03766.

ACKNOWLEDGMENTS

The author wishes to thank the following journals in which the poems listed below first appeared, some in different form:

The American Voice	Ever
	Great Pond
Choice	Little Fingers
Confrontation	Giving In
Gulf Coast	Nude Hugging Her Own
Ironwood	Metropolitan Poem
	On the Eve of the Bombing
	With One Hand Missing
Lips	Christmas in Germany
Pequod	Big Spring
	The Issue
Poetry	It Was a Story
	Night and Day
	Station Music
	The Room
	The Silence
	The Tunnel
	This Morning
The Poetry Review	This Life
	Your Own Good Leg
TriQuarterly	Still Life

The author also wishes to acknowledge the New York Foundation for the Arts for its support.

This book is for Helena

CONTENTS

I call heaven and earth to witness against you this day,
that I have set before you life and death, blessing and curse;
therefore choose life, that you and your descendants may live.

Deuteronomy 30.19

DEAR READER

It's you
I've been waiting for

LITTLE FINGERS

For Mom and Are

When I was born I weighed nine pounds
eight ounces; that was the last time
I was heavy—so heavy my mother
could only haul me to the third-floor
landing where Grandma met her
to carry me the next two flights.

When I was a boy Grandma played
a game with me. She hid her hands
behind her back, and I had to guess
which hand held the penny. If I
guessed right, she kissed me twice
on the cheek. At age four
I was convinced I was a genius.

There's a photo of me,
grinning, standing naked on Grandpa's
knees, wearing his crumpled rain hat.
I'm holding a box of Lux detergent
as if I was doing an ad for the soap.
My mother is pointing at me and laughing.

In grade school I was short and skinny,
always first on line with taller boys
behind me. There were kids on my block

who could punch a ball over a six-story building,
even a kid with palsied fingers who became
a handball champion. There are no excuses.

Once my friends pinned me against
a chain-link fence and one by one
they slammed me. The funny thing is
I made no effort to stop them.
They could have hit me another hour.

I'm tall now but very skinny. When I look
at photos of myself, wearing swim trunks,
leaning forward, I think if someone breathed
lightly, I'd topple over. My students
laugh at me. They point and call me
Skinny Figgy. On field trips they drink beer
and vomit out the school bus window.
One kid, for no reason, threw a book
that hit me in the middle of my forehead.

I feel nothing. I didn't cry when Grandpa
died; I've never bled black eye shadow
like the woman I love who cries when I say
I love her, when I'm really planning
tomorrow's lessons. I feel like a slim digit
zipping through computers; I move so fast
I'm always missing.

My father isn't skinny. He does one hundred
push-ups a day and makes his biceps dance
the hula. When I was a boy we bathed together;
he rubbed my legs with a soft red towel.
He played with me in hotel swimming pools,
dumping Dixie cups of water over my head,
then lifting me to his shoulders
so all the neighbors could see his son.

Maybe that's why I love water, and fountains—
the elegant marble drinking fountain
in Grand Central Station, and the more common
square-cut fountains in the playgrounds
of the boroughs. I hate water that comes out
cool and thin, like the water from aluminum
fountains in the hallways of large corporations.
I like it sweet and thick, big around
as a finger. When I drink that water
I'm in the middle of a long deep kiss.

Most of all I love the ocean—throwing myself
against the waves that rise ten feet above my head.
I love staring them down as they rear back,
then going under and coming up, my lungs
bloated with air. I laugh at the ocean,
the biggest thing I know in the world,
because the waves can knock me down,
but I still rise and ride them.

I remember watching my father swim laps,
once around a small pool every ten minutes.
He swam so slow I thought each stroke
would be his last, and he'd freeze
with one arm raised above the water's surface.

I want to move that slow and gather weight
around me. I want my little fingers back,
the ones that gripped the bars of my crib
when I struggled to stand and shook them
when I was hungry. No more pinned
against a fence. No more disappearing.
That's why I'm telling you this—
because the words are like fingers
inside me, they rub against me
like fingers smudging glass, and the fingers
and the smudges convince me that I'm here.

I.

THE ISSUE

My psychiatrist says the issue is intimacy—
the issue is rage and how it finds its target.
It is a small room and both of us in it.
How many sleep alone, counting a coleus or a TV
as their best friend? I wonder how we give up blame;
I search the real estate pages hoping for a home
to save us. Nothing will save us, not even a home
and not my psychiatrist with his theories on intimacy—
how it builds back slowly, how first you touch a hand,
a neck, remembering how you once woke, each stroking
the long side of the other, how there were hours
instead of issues, and the length and warmth of your body,
the shift of your legs, the rise of your perfume, the way
you shook the bracelet down your arm and did that thing
with your tongue—yes, the rapid pull toward each other
was that day's issue—the finger-lock, toe-lock, smell of neck,
the ache which ground the bits of us whole, which found us
silent and alert, under each other's wing, the saving grace
or need that scraped the bitter taste from our tongues.

NOT GETTING ANY

of that
girl
boy
on the counter
leaning back
getting lots
of polished
thighs
see through
sheer sheen
wafer thin
formulaic muscle math
greased glow
poke spin
not now
when

ONE TREE

It wasn't that she lacked an essence,
or was treated any less harshly—
it was an accident, a strength she had.
A smacks B whacks C—that's why she reacted.
Anyone can love anyone; the race is to the ego.
Consider the palm tree which no one considers.

In a strange city, not one car will stop.
Or the one that does is loaded with danger.
Meanwhile, the palm trees change direction.
In the city of her discontent she writes a letter.
A five-year something comes to an end
with no more drama than a boy scraping his knee.

Remember the beauty of conversation?
Tables. Trees. Sitting under one, you realize
it was a long time ago—that image of a man
eating something, a flight of stairs, you
staring at the you upon it. Belief is a song
recited to oneself. Under one tree.

OTHERWISE

how to describe
the
off balance so
everyone will know
such a knot of
disappointed
yes I'm losing
your personal
myth about
the value of a wall
without which
we'd just look back
what we lack
walking down
the further
side of wrong

IT WAS A STORY

It was a story about hair,
about a blue chair and solitude,
about years and how years pass,
from one day into a future.

It was a story about trees,
about something as simple
as finding a tree, or a leaf
fallen from a tree in summer.

It was a tale about a green
lamp and leaning over,
how everything falls and there
are moments—it was a moment,

an elongation under the elms,
when I felt the heart
was fraught with danger—
one day it simply misfires,

you're under a blanket
or pressed back into
a chair, and all that's left
is a vague impression,

a blue solitude, and the life
you imagined has suddenly
vanished. What's remembered
is lost and will not reappear,

although there is this body
when all the trees have gone,
and the sky is cold and full
of crows I cannot see or hear.

AWAY

The idea
of disintegration
was enough
to get me
out of the house.

I was happy
between my
own two walls—
away from you,
an edge in air,

I stared in windows,
opened books,
took my body to bed.
Back at the ranch
more misery

brewed, everything
was covered,
there was no air.
I remember it
all, how sad

we were, how
we turned each
other cold. And
we would have it
no other way.

ONCE

You missed me that day and called from the station;
your voice was saying everything I wanted—
I lay down and let the words pass over.

A short time after, sadness took over—
lectures, pacing, and sighing;
the deeds I did were unsatisfying.

Outside the leaves were brilliantly turning;
we forgot ourselves, enjoyed the show,
then one day we let go.

THE TUNNEL

If you dig down deep enough
and lose the world of light
and let yourself descend
in the thick tunnel of air
and forget what it was like
to learn the outline of a hill
or breast, if you allow the pressure
of the narrowing walls, down
where you must wedge in, out of sight,
and settle in the damp cusp, the first home,
the air which stinks of grease, and read
what's written on the tunnel wall
and cannot find your name, if you dig where
there is no grip, no face, neither
friend nor foe, where the bones
which once knew the logic of your chest
scatter like thrown sticks—
there you'll wait for the good push,
the fierce act, that gives you up
and sets the tunnel aflame.

THE NEW POEM

will not entertain us
will not move quickly

will not look handsome
will not wear a tie

will not hesitate
will not understand

will rescue no one

STILL LIFE

I take the objects I love and arrange them—

brown egg
white pitcher
yellow bowl circled
with periwinkle blue

All objects find their home;
all objects are seated.

All pose—like Aunt Martha
with Aunt Rose—the early, formal days.

The elegant cup casts an elegant shadow.

Who's to say the love of objects
pales beside the love of people.

The objects on the table are so peaceful;
I think about their lives.

The mind arranges itself
endlessly, slowly—

it will put the bowl
wherever it wants.

And who is looking at me?
What finite place is mine?

GREAT POND

If you take this
and you carve it out
with a sharp knife
and make sure
it's cut clean
and it will hold
like a raft in water
like a well-made raft
and you can stand
you're set in the sun
it has your name
there is no confusion
and you feel no shame
floating there
away from them
and you wave
and love them
even as you leave
but keep your balance
your love of water
and move intact
further out
until you cannot
see them—
the shoreline fades
it's all sky
all water
you've got the raft

you trust your hand
then you sail
past the rocking boats
past the little island
then you really lose them
then you will be happy

YOUR OWN GOOD LEG

You wake to your right leg gone;
you don't know who did it,
you didn't feel it happen,
but there's the ragged cut line.
Your leg lies next to you;
you can feel the warmth
still in it. You rest your head
on its knee and notice
for the first time what a wonderful
leg it is, even its hairy calf
and skinny ankle. It stares at you,
you who were dreaming your life
was whole, when it wasn't.

The moral of the story is:
life is serious, legs are lost;
it's all in a night's work
to those who come hacking.
Your own good leg is gone;
you caress the left one, still
breathing, alive and lonely.

O TO THE RIVER OF WORDS

Having said it he felt better.
But, it only took courage.
Correct, he said, corrected.
Consequently he tasted freedom.
Only the absence of speech rebuked him.
Rooted in belief he spoke it.
Inside the word was power.
Put another way, it transformed him.
Happy in the knowledge it was spoken.
Specifically, he nailed it.
Inches away from silence.

THE SILENCE

In memory of my father, William Figman

My father's hand sits in a bowl of soup;
his sleeve is covered with grease.
He's lost his hair, except for the gray tuft
behind his head where they sliced
through the bone with a small electric
saw, then pieced his skull together.

I remember how I rode him, how he bucked
through the house, my Wild Mouse, my Twister.
After his morning shower, he smoothed his thick
black curls, sprinkled his toes with powder,
and when he brushed water from his chest,
and wrapped a towel around his middle,
I got the first whiff of the body I was growing.

Father was silent at dinner, silent as he sharpened
two knives above his head then sliced through
the back of a chicken. What rage he felt,
that made his cheeks flush red, he never spoke it.
He chewed past the meat into the marrow;
his silence left a hole that made me wobble.

Now he moans for his wallet and his watch,
his wallet tucked in his pajama pocket,
gold watches on both wrists. Papa, I slide

three almonds across the table to wish you health;
I would press my palms to the ache in your head,
wipe the tumor clean, but each day
you grow more silent and sleep an extra hour.

ON THE EVE OF THE BOMBING

Father has no heart.
He is all the shattered air.

Whose eyes are sealed with prayer?
And who still kisses the head of the Blessed Virgin?

Small brown birds rain from the sky,
Deader than the chocolate eggs we ate last Easter.

We pull the lost sailor's white hat
Over the eyes of his daughter.

The sky is split by silver planes
Raced by men wearing leather.

They find their targets,
Lower their noses.

Where is the thrust to right it all,
The dark song within your body?

It is a long time gone,
Sterner than a cemetery.

Father is a bloated head bobbing in green water.
He smiles at us,

Making the sign of the cross
In the air which offers no resistance—

Now praise the first gold heads of the crocus,
The pink and white sleeves of magnolia.

Now kneel down in that field
With a black bone wedged

Between your jaws, and speak
What you must speak softly.

II.

NIGHT AND DAY

The richness of the evening is in the evening,
the steam hissing, the breath rising in you
like old steam, like the end, finally,
of a long winter, or long illness, like touch
between two people, finally mastered,
like the death of manners, the laying on
of real lashes, like your life running
into the room, a messenger, out of breath,
too happy to breathe, falling to the floor
and lying there, the morning passing through it,
a ridge of sun refusing to be broken,
a head rising between two hills that govern
the city, which just goes on, ignoring the message.

The richness of the day lies in the folds
of her dress, the sweet lemon taste
on the tip of her tongue, which now
she offers, as she steps up to you,
the distance between you fully absorbed,
a way in which day and evening merge,
you do not notice the ease of fusion,
which just goes on as the city goes on,
oblivious to you, and your place in it.

EVER

spring it is the very
best of very every
berry every mother

tree dips in such
a lovely hats off
the proper

every head turns
to watch what
breezes down in spring

every helpful
boy leaves
every button open

every stubborn branch
every sticky stick
every branch lit with leaves

leaves young ever
everybody knows
spring will never end

ever

RIDING IN

raven hair
held by
a silver pin
something turn
of century about
the elegant curve
of cheek
the way she
turns easily
away her small
hand gripping
the bright chromium
pole a raspberry
scarf wound
loosely round
her neck she
will say
nothing I
will say
nothing back
as she moves
through the door
a lovely
white boat lifted
by a gentle wave
gently further out

STATION MUSIC

I wanted to crawl into it, become the bird of that music,
and float like white feathers in the dark subway station.
I wanted to plant myself like a sincere kiss from red lips
on the forehead of that strange woman who listened in a long
black coat, in wet boots. I wanted the week to come to a calm end,
harming no one, like a road that ends in soft, orange leaves.
I wanted to be a calloused finger easing a few slow notes from that
seductive sax or pulling a few taut strings. I wanted to miss the next train
and keep on listening, the music climbing the poles of the station,
infecting my feet, circling like a bee above a hammock—it was summer,
make no mistake, it was slow and summer, it was syrup flowing,
thick grass blowing, it was all this in their lips and fingers,
it was the weaving of the sax and strings, like a hand in fur,
like a fur coat bristling, like a woman in black fur sitting down
to a white table, licking a spoon loaded with raspberries,
like a red fox alert in a field of snow, like a field that goes on awhile
in its own rhythm, a field that resolves beyond the barn, like hay
stacked neatly, like good hay aging, like farm boys growing strong,
a low whistle late in the afternoon, the feeding done, the hunger
rising in their bellies, their tough hands washed under warm water,
it was their day, they made their mark, and now this music,
far from them, this train to take us home, the long way in it.

THIS LIFE

I'm chasing a train
and my life is on it,
my life on that train,
the doors are closing.

I poke my arms through—
I will not let that train leave,
not with my life on it.

I grab it and walk down the platform,
balancing my life on my head,
graceful as the Haitian women
walking their baskets of fruit.

I balance it well,
I feel its weight,
I smile at my life,
my best friend,
the one I save again.

CHRISTMAS IN GERMANY

I see the girls
twisting their hair in braids,
remembering nothing of the war—

I watch them march
down the aisle
in white and red robes,

and I am moved by their voices,
their round
vulnerable mouths.

POEM

Pear, apple, plate
Solid, piece, blue
Paint, canvas, tight
Cross, blue, pair
Pear, bite, jewel
Apple, hips, rose
Bottle, lit, to
You, flying, home

THE ROOM

Friend, I speak to you
in ways I never intended

When you brush against me
move into view
stand by a machine
sit across the room
show me your fingers
untie your shoe

it excites me

I look forward to seeing you
in ways I never expected—

the people outside this room
would never guess

just as I never guessed

THIS MORNING

I am no longer meeting with losers
Those who carry on over long drinks
About what they are not doing
Those with endless explanations
Full of detail

Here is the first step that knows
Where the next step is going
The necktie that rings with authority
The first splash of water over my lips

At last the rain is coming
A crop which will not fail me
New leaves poking through ecstatic branches

And women in white dresses
Whose soft pleats hold the light
On my side of the street
This fine and friendly morning

GIVING IN

For Ella

I love how the hay
sticks out of our shirts,
we cannot keep it in, the hay
has its own mind, forget
we were embarrassed. The air
sweeps under your blouse,
your skin rises to greet it.
I love how you lean back
and how your body lengthens,
how this moment lengthens,
until there is no time and time
is all around us. I love
how we give in, we cannot help
this slow roll, this fall
into each other, into
the evening around us.

METROPOLITAN POEM

I was hungry, hungry and not eating,
I was hungry, and she was there,
with her mouth which was open, her legs
which rubbed against me, she was there,
with a cup of water, with great
plates of food, and I was eating,
not like a pig, but slow and steady

(a room in the middle
of the city, the cars many floors below, tiny
islands of light, the people in the cars
talking or sleeping, listening to the radio,
unhappy or whistling, returning from parties
or heading to work, the cars were gliding,
many stories high, I ate from her hand,
I finished eating)

and then sleeping,
she turned in her sleep, the color of her hair
was brown, ordinary brown, I saw the red highlights,
she was sleeping gently, exhausted, wearing her summer
nightgown, and one breast slid out,
the nipple soft and sleeping

NIGHTSPEED

O baby it's back
Necktie
Purple
Long slope
Little mountain
Precious cherry
The snow they buried
Was warm
And you slid
The thin socks
Such a body
Stacked together
Two cradles
Two sleds
Behind the curtain
The red bodysuit
O perilous body
O young impossible body

NUDE HUGGING HER OWN

When you think of her,
you think of red licorice
and what champagne
does to the body;
you think of weakness
in the legs, and falling
and dying, all the little mouths
on the moonscape of her neck—
you think of black kerchiefs,
a warm round sun,
a clear body of water.

And if she breaks
the surface of the pond
and comes back to you
wet from head to toe,
that's a brand new coat
for you to wear.
And if she leans back
and gives herself completely
to the blue ceiling,
she becomes the nude
hugging her own,
emptied of pleasure.

RUBY

Ruby of my eye and one good squeeze,
wrap me up I'm happy.
My mind keeps wandering off—
Ruby's the bone that pulls me back,
the white steam I wrap myself in,
my shawl for quiet meditation.

Ruby red delicious jam—
what matters is your open mouth,
the concentration of your left hand—
you offer me your shoulder!

Happy I could be this happy
occurs to me as I eat more,
dip deeply into melon,
the essential facts lost at last,
my mind a burst of pure white vapor.

Lord praise the tongue
that knows its business—
red was delicious,
Ruby in my mouth was tender;

pinkness was my perfect fish,
the closing of a dear book,
a dream down in darkness where
we live so brightly
there is no danger—

only a tree blazing,
one thousand new leaves waving,
a sweetness born of cider,
a maple tapped completely—

Ruby, I was in that tree
and swaying; you are what makes
a glum boy glow—look, we have
a new bird at our window.

WITH ONE HAND MISSING

                    to sail up
with one fist clenched, to speak one's name believe it,
to thrust out in summer air disturbed by the scent
of one young woman

                    you attack the waves,
you mean to make a pain of yourself,
you who are incensed with the flesh

of she who walks the beach nude, who binds her own
kind of pain into the eyes of we who assert our right to gaze

                    yes, the trick is laughter, the trick is a hoot the length
of this long beach, the trick is you are not leaving—

you with one hand gone, but one hand whole,
dumb excited hand, brother of the starfish,
that has no mind, that simply holds and knows

she walks the beach as if she owns it—

O glorious hand, see
how proudly she is walking

VOW

in serious in gladness

in claiming in strength

in fallow in fearsome

in follow in mend

in mired in madness

in many in leaf

in languish in years

in lonely in need

in sequel in sessions

in lessons in fall

in tantrum in tainted

in failure in walls

in woeful in forward

in patience in fence

in risen in fated

in favor in yes

BIG SPRING

For Henry Kellerman

The sun is breaking through the window
in incandescent flashes, but you say
it's no big deal. All you know is the steam
in our pipes keeps on kicking. The magnolias
have opened their arms to greet us, the sun
circles closer to our planet, but you still feel
a chill in the air—as far as you're concerned
it's just another spin around the axis, it's no
big spring, nothing that enormous. Last night
I dreamed of a squad of shortstops oiling the stiffness
out of their gloves—the smell of pine tar
sometimes flies all the way from Pensacola,
but no green diamond, not even Central Park
with its banks of azaleas scrubbed by last night's rain
convinces you to savor this season. Let it die,
you say, let it pass as everything passes. But I
insist precisely since this spring will pass
that we must hold it as we might hold a last splash
of water. It's spring and the sun butters every rooftop
in this city and the bleached concrete and the bricks
dyed a brighter shade of salmon. Sunlight soaks the long
trembling legs of women jogging by the river, the sweat
that sprouts behind their knees sweet as rain dripping
down the maples. Beautiful this noon and the tipping
of the season, its appearance and its disappearing, this big
fat spring, this ample space between, this moment shuddering open.

Elliot Figman was born and raised in the Bronx and was educated at Oberlin College and the University of Massachusetts. He taught in Massachusetts and Brooklyn before coming to Poets & Writers where he now serves as Executive Director. A recipient of a New York Foundation for the Arts Poetry Fellowship, he has published his work in *Pequod, Poetry, TriQuarterly,* and other literary journals. He lives in Manhattan with his wife, Ella.

Photo: Ella Figman

"Elliot Figman's poems are ecstatic in the origina the best, sense of the word. They stand out fror themselves, and by doing so they give to th transparent human ardors and longings tha inspire them a disquieting luminousness. The bring us, by means of their faultless elegance an their clarifying order, face to face with th astonishing paradox that only by cherishing wha is within the reach of our hands and present to ou eyes can we transcend the boundaries of ou world. All the poems in *Big Spring* are beautifu and many of them are almost unbearably so."

— Vijay Seshadri

"Praise is the abundant impulse behind Ellio Figman's *Big Spring*. For Figman, praise is no simply the product of the world whose fields hol 'the first gold heads of the crocus, / The pink an white sleeves of magnolia.' In Figman's univers praise is the result of having knelt 'down in tha field / With a black bone wedged // Between you jaws, [to] speak / What you must speak softly. Readers will find much to *praise* in these direc clear, and softly spoken poems for they remind u of the quiet and authentic urgency at the heart o lyric poetry."

— Michael Collier

"Meditative, playful, sensual, and witty, Ellio Figman's poems offer us insights and mysterie that veer from the cool, precise ruminations o loss to lyrical intensities of joy...What begins in a exploration of sorrow and restraint ends in reso nance and amplitude, all the while acknowledgin an unbiased universe. It is exhilarating to rea these evolved and varied poems of transformatio and love."

—Colette Inez

ISBN 1-884800-47-5
51495>
9 781884 800474

US$14.9

A Stahlecker Series Selectio

Four Way Books/ Poetr

www.fourwaybooks.con